Settle to Carlisle:
An Artist's Odyssey

Les Packham

Published by Northern Arts Publications
an imprint of Jeremy Mills Publishing Limited

113 Lidget Street
Lindley
Huddersfield
West Yorkshire HD3 3JR

www.jeremymillspublishing.co.uk

First published 2013
Text and images © Les Packham

ISBN 978-1-906600-92-1

Front cover: *Ribblehead Viaduct* © Les Packham

In memory of my grandfather, Joseph Arthur
Bradwell, and my uncle, Jack Pennington,
for sowing the seeds.

Contents

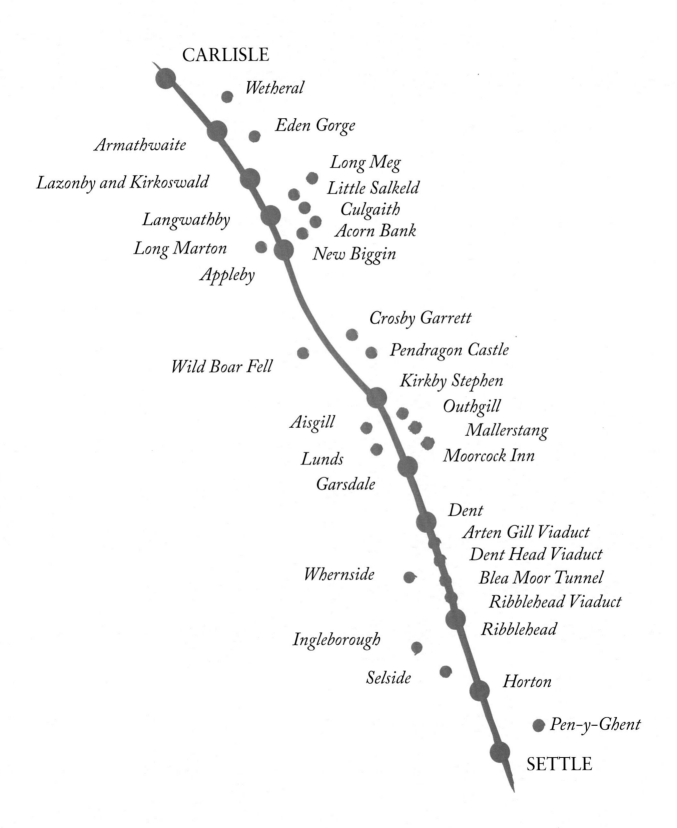

CARLISLE

Wetheral

Eden Gorge

Armathwaite

Lazonby and Kirkoswald

Long Meg

Little Salkeld

Culgaith

Langwathby

Acorn Bank

Long Marton

New Biggin

Appleby

Crosby Garrett

Pendragon Castle

Wild Boar Fell

Kirkby Stephen

Outhgill

Aisgill

Mallerstang

Lunds

Moorcock Inn

Garsdale

Dent

Arten Gill Viaduct

Dent Head Viaduct

Whernside

Blea Moor Tunnel

Ribblehead Viaduct

Ribblehead

Ingleborough

Selside

Horton

Pen-y-Ghent

SETTLE

Preston's Folly, Settle

Foreword

I first met Les Packham when we were both police officers in West Yorkshire. The force had the good sense to recognise his talents and he was in effect the force artist. For some reason I found myself posted to ancient police stations which were about to be replaced by magnificent and huge new ones. Conscious of the heritage that was about to be lost and aware of the power or the artist over that of the photographer, I asked Les to record the old police stations at Wortley, Pudsey and Halifax. I still have, and treasure, prints of those early 'Packhams'.

For five years I was Chairman of the Friends of the Settle-Carlisle Line (FoSCL) the organisation set up in the early 1980s to oppose the then very real threat of closure of the line. It is therefore a double delight to have been asked to write this foreword.

The views from the train windows are superb but as this book so vividly illustrates it does not stop there. Get off at any of the stations and there are treats aplenty around every corner.

Having had the privilege of a preview of all the scenes I declare that Les Packham has captured the spirit of the line and its scenery to perfection. A piece on the USA's ABC news channel a couple of years ago put the Settle-Carlisle Line in the top two of the world's greatest rail journeys. The following pages give spectacular glimpses as to why.

Mark Rand

Former Chairman of the Friends
of the Settle–Carlisle Line (FoSCL)

Joseph Arthur Bradwell, born 4th January 1882.
Photograph taken summer 1899 on commencement of
employment with Midland Railway.

Introduction

This book makes no pretence of providing a history of the railway line from Settle to Carlisle. This has already been done several times and far more eloquently than I could ever do. Indeed, this book is an evocative journey that encapsulates the mood and atmosphere of the countryside surrounding the Settle-Carlisle line.

My interest began as a small boy of perhaps eight or nine when, during the school holidays, my parents would place me in the care of the guard of the express from St Pancras to Leeds or Bradford, where a relative would meet me and I would spend my school holidays in Keighley. This trust in the said guard no doubt stemmed from the fact that my maternal grandfather Joseph Arthur Bradwell had joined the Midland Railway in 1899, becoming a guard later in his service. He retired on the last day of 1947 – the day before the railways were nationalised. I have no idea whether he actually worked on the Settle-Carlisle Line but it would be nice to think that he did.

My first recollection of the line was just a year or two later when, in the company of a favourite uncle, we embarked on various walks in the Dales. He was extremely knowledgeable about transport and I have fond memories of sitting on a hillside (possibly Pen-y-ghent) in glorious sunshine, eating our potted meat teacakes and drinking orange juice as he explained to me the mechanical intricacies of the 'Royal Scot' class locomotive in the process of heaving its load up to Aisgill, its three cylinder exhaust reverberating off the hillsides. I was well into my teens before I actually travelled over the whole of the line.

I didn't start painting until later in life and, being partly inspired by the Dales scenery, it wasn't long before I was reintroduced to the Settle to Carlisle line. Painting – along with my other interest, motorcycling – soon had me exploring the environment surrounding the line and sowed a seed that one day I would like to do a book on the area. Here it is!

Settle to Carlisle

Settle

*The River Ribble,
Settle*

The little market town of Settle was bypassed several years ago but is still the major centre of the central southern Dales. It is constantly busy with walkers, visitors to the railway and people having business in the town or the surrounding area. Settle is dominated by its market square which still holds its weekly market after 750 years. The Shambles, the old open market arcade, retains its shops and provides the famous backdrop to the square. Tanner Hall constructed by Robert Preston in 1675 is more familiarly known as Preston's Folly and stands not too far away.

Giggleswick

Across the railway line to the west of Settle stands the village of Giggleswick, whose main claim to fame is its public school. Founded in 1512, the school received its charter in 1553. Near the school on a raised area of land stands the Grade II listed chapel. Completed in 1901 to commemorate the Diamond Jubilee of Queen Victoria, it was built to the designs of T. G. Jackson. The unusual copper dome is a landmark for miles around. It has been cleaned in recent years as part of a restoration programme started in 1995. The late Graham Watson MA MBE, who was chairman of the governors for many years, was instrumental in replacing the dreadful 1960s strip lighting with accurate copies of the original gas mantles.

Giggleswick

School Chapel,
Giggleswick

Langcliffe

It was after the rededication of the new lighting that the BBC programme 'Songs of Praise' was held at the chapel and the television lighting showed the magnificent mosaic work of the interior of the dome. Staggered by the beauty of the mosaics, Watson paid for hidden lighting to be installed so that the beauty of the interior of the dome could be enjoyed for years to come.

Langcliffe

Travelling north out of Settle towards Horton-in-Ribblesdale, a mile or so up the road the first community encountered is Langcliffe. A small, typical Dales village with a Victorian church, the houses cluster round the village green. Langcliffe seems to get overlooked in books about Yorkshire, so I thought I would redress the balance a little with this painting, one of many possibilities in the village.

Stainforth Force

Just below the packhorse bridge the river Ribble cascades over a series of limestone steps. Known as Stainforth Force, this spot, attractive on a calm day, can turn into a malevolent maelstrom after heavy rain.

The packhorse bridge replaced an earlier structure dating back to the fourteenth century, which in turn had superseded a 'stony ford' (Stainforth). In bygone days this crossing was part of the drove road which ran between York and Lancaster.

Three Peaks

Clustered together on the western fringes of the Dales lies Yorkshire's famous Three Peaks, each of them made from shale and limestone surmounted by millstone grit. The highest at 2414ft, but probably the least spectacular, is Whernside, a long, lumbering length of hill which provides the massive backdrop to Ribblehead Viaduct. It is least spectacular, too, in as much as it boasts fewer attractions in the way of gills, caves and potholes than the other two peaks.

Flat-topped Ingleborough at 2373ft is the second highest of the peaks and the most westerly of the three, its distinctive shape visible for miles. I have painted it on many occasions and it seems that whenever I do and from whatever angle, it is always in shadow. Unlike Whernside, Ingleborough has more than its fair share of potholes and caves. Probably the most famous is Gaping Gill, with its huge chamber reputed to be the largest in the world. Others are also impressive, including Alum Pot, Hurnel Moss Pot and Lancaster Hole, to mention just a few.

Unlike Ingleborough, Pen-y-ghent (2273ft) always appears to be swathed in sunshine. On a recent, very wet visit to Settle, Pen-y-ghent could be seen in the distance in all its sunlit glory. It has a shape not dissimilar to Ingleborough but with a more rounded profile and its position in the landscape seems more exposed. Walkers and fell runners preparing to tackle the Three Peaks from Horton in Ribblesdale usually start with Pen-y-ghent, followed by Whernside and completing the trio with Ingleborough. On average walkers complete the trek in ten to twelve hours for the twenty-three mile round trip, whereas experienced fell runners can manage it in around four.

Selside

Selside is a picturesque hamlet just to the north of Horton in Ribblesdale. An old signal box sign nailed to a barn wall proclaims the location of this community.

Selside

The ghost of Big John was often seen in the vicinity of the signal box although it is not known who Big John actually was. In snowy weather, although his apparition can be clearly seen, it is reputed to leave no footprints. From the west a fine view of Pen-y-ghent, the third highest of the Yorkshire peaks, and arguably the most attractive, can be seen across the village and the railway tracks.

Ribblehead

Of all the structures on the Settle and Carlisle line, Ribblehead Viaduct is by far the most iconic and famous. It is not the most attractive viaduct on the line – that plaudit probably goes to Arten Gill – nor the highest; that's Smardale. It is, however, the longest. But what makes it is its position. Majestic and proud, its twenty-four arches stride magnificently across Batty Moss as if to say, 'Look at me – aren't I great!'

In the early 1990s the poor condition of the viaduct was the reason given to condemn the Settle and Carlisle line altogether. It was also the catalyst for a campaign to save it that ultimately proved successful.

Pen-y-ghent from Horton-in-Ribblesdale

Chapel-le-Dale

*St Leonard's Church,
Chapel-le-Dale*

*Inglebrough from
Chapel-le-Dale*

Chapel Le Dale

A book such as this must feature the Parish Church of St Leonards. This tiny church nestles quietly in a peaceful setting overlooked by the bulk of Ingleborough and welcomes visitors to take a look inside. Most people who are interested in the line can come here to pay their respects to the 200 men, women and children who died from injury or disease during the construction of the Ribblehead Viaduct and who are buried here. It is worth spending time on the bench beside the door in quiet reflection and to enjoy the peace of the surroundings.

Arten Gill

Dent Head Viaduct, Arten Gill and Dentdale

Travelling north on the Settle and Carlisle line one bursts forth from Blea Moor tunnel on to Dent Head viaduct. The view of Dentdale to the west is, in my mind, the most stunning on the whole line. This view continues as the train traverses the handsome Arten Gill viaduct on its way to Dent station. My paintings show Dent Head viaduct from the road that ultimately drops down under the second arch. This is a well known view but its composition is worth reproducing here.

The pretty hamlet of Arten Gill with the viaduct in the background was a must to paint and a short walk up the lane shows the viaduct in its full splendour. Built of Dent 'marble' quarried locally, it consists of eleven arches of tapering columns and stands 117 feet high.

Arten Gill Viaduct

The wide sweep in the painting of Dentdale was painted from near Dent station, which isn't exactly convenient for the community with the village being four and a half miles away. The first time I attempted it, it had to be abandoned due to a huge plague of flying ants; however, a little later in the year, the conditions produced the painting seen here.

Dent Head Viaduct

Garsdale

When the line was built in the 1870s, Garsdale station was originally known as Hawes junction because of the divergence of a single line to the town of Hawes almost six miles away. There is no real community of Garsdale Head apart from a couple of farms and a few cottages built by the railway to house its workers.

Garsdale itself is a fertile, wooded valley that runs westwards from Garsdale head at its watershed with Wensleydale towards Sedbergh. Here once were a number of Viking settlements, one of which is the only real community in Garsdale and is known as 'The Street'.

Ruswarp

Ruswarp the Border Collie cross was the constant companion of Graham Nuttall, one of the founder members of the Friends of the Settle to Carlisle Preservation Group which was formed in 1981. Being a fare-paying passenger, Ruswarp (pronounced Russup) had a valid vote in the petition raised to save the line. Graham was a keen fell walker and whilst walking in the Welsh mountains went missing on 20th January 1990. His neighbours raised the alarm and, despite extensive searching by police and fell rescue organisations, neither were found for eleven weeks. Graham had died, but his faithful companion Ruswarp, though barely alive, had remained by his master's side. Ruswarp was in a poor state but was nursed back to survive long enough to attend Graham's funeral. Sadly, he died the following day.

Following a letter in a newspaper an appeal was launched to provide a statue to commemorate the life of the dog and his master and on 11th April 2009 a bronze sculpture of Ruswarp by the eminent sculptress Joel Walker was unveiled on Garsdale Station, a favourite location of the pair.

Ruswarp

Moorcock Inn and Lunds

Lunds Viaduct

School Cottages at Lunds

The Moorcock Inn lies on the A684 Hawes to Sedbergh road at its junction with the B6259, within sight of Dandry Mire viaduct and Moorcock tunnel. The road to Kirkby Stephen runs parallel with the railway for most of its length. At Lunds, a small settlement of a few houses and a school, can be seen the short five-arch viaduct, just north of which was the scene of the 1910 railway disaster on the climb to Ais Gill.

The Moorcock Inn

View towards Sedburgh

Pendragon Castle

Pendragon Castle

Whatever you have heard or read about Pendragon Castle being built by Uther Pendragon, father of King Arthur, it is no more than fanciful legend. Pendragon was built by Hugh de Morville of Brough and Appleby castles fame sometime between 1175 and 1180, when it was probably known as Mallvestang Castle (later the Castle of Mallerstang). It was believed to have been originally constructed of wood and it was burnt down by the raiding Scots in the mid-fourteenth century. It was rebuilt and in 1541 was again destroyed by fire but this time accidentally.

1643 saw it passed to Lady Anne Clifford, Countess of Pembroke, who rebuilt it yet again and visited it frequently. During the 1680s it was dismantled by the Earl of Thanet, who occupied it after Anne's death. More recently Lord Hothfield gave the site to English Heritage and today more restoration is taking place.

Mallerstang and Outhgill

Mallerstang Dale is dominated on its eastern side by Mallerstang Edge which nowhere along its length falls below 2000 feet in height. Whilst to the west, Wild Boar Fell dominates. The hamlet of Outhgill retains its old Norse scattering of homes and farms and my painting shows the route through the village from Moorcock to Kirkby Stephen.

St Mary's Church in the village has a dedication to the twenty-five men, women and children buried there who perished during the building of the Mallerstang stretch of the line.

Outhgill

Wild Boar Fell, Mallerstang

Crosby Garrett

Brough Castle

Brough

Crosby Garrett

Crosby Garrett railway station, which was built alongside the viaduct, was closed in 1956. A small farming community, Crosby Garrett is dominated by St Andrew's Church which boasts an Anglo Saxon chancel.

The village's most recent claim to fame is the discovery of a rare, ceremonial Roman helmet, one of only three of its kind found so far in Britain.

Brough Castle

Brough Castle lies about nine miles south east of Appleby and is easily seen from the A66. It was originally built by William II in 1093 on the site of a Roman fort and was given to the Scots in 1136 who held it until 1157 when it came under the English Crown – but not for long. It was granted to Hugh de Morville who built the three storey keep, but in 1173 it was once again confiscated by the Scots, who virtually destroyed it the following year. It was then held by the Crown from 1190 until 1203, when it was granted to a nephew of de Morville, Robert de Vieuxpont, by King John. Come 1269 and it passed to the Clifford family, who occupied it until 1251. That year it was set on fire and remained a ruin until Lady Anne Clifford restored it in 1661 but after her death it once more fell into disrepair. In 1928 however, it was presented to what is now English Heritage.

*Appleby Bridge over
the River Eden*

*Clapper Bridge, near
Crosby Garrett*

Long Marton

Appleby

Formerly the county town of Westmoreland, Appleby's main industry is now tourism, partly because of its interesting town and its attractive location in a loop of the river Eden.

Appleby Castle dates from the twelfth century, having being founded by Ranulf le Mechines. In the mid-seventeenth century like many other castles in the area Appleby castle was owned by Lady Anne Clifford, who restored it, and again like Brough and Pendragon it passed to the Earls of Thanet on her death.

One of Appleby's more famous attractions is the annual gypsy horse fair which is held during the first week in June. It dates back to a charter granted in 1685 by James II and is held on Fair (formerly Gallows) Hill on the outskirts of the town. It attracts up to 10,000 gypsies/travellers who come to celebrate their lifestyle and trade horses. Up to 30,000 visitors descend on Appleby that week to view the spectacle.

In a previous life I had the brief pleasure of meeting the Rt Rev. Eric Treacy MBE when he was Bishop of Wakefield. A passionate railway enthusiast, he became one of the foremost railway photographers of his era and was affectionately known as the Railway Bishop. On 13th May 1978, whilst waiting to join a railtour Eric Treacy collapsed and died from a heart attack on Appleby Station. A blue wall plaque adorns the station and a preserved steam locomotive was named after him in his honour.

Temple Sowerby and Dorothy Una Ratcliffe

Dorothy Una Ratcliffe, who became known by her initials DUR, was born in Brighton in 1887 and became a prolific author and poet inspired by the Yorkshire dialect. She eventually became President of the Yorkshire Dialect Society in

1963–4. Most of her books were illustrated and many featured the work of well-known Yorkshire artist Fred Lawson.

Dorothy was married three times but it was her second husband, Captain Noel McGrigor Phillips, whom she described as the love of her life. Temple Sowerby Manor was purchased by them and was later called Acorn Bank. Crowdundle Beck, known locally as Croodle Beck, ran through the estate and this turned the waterwheel for Acorn Bank. Dorothy and Noel had extensive repairs done to the house and planted thousands of daffodils in the grounds. They travelled extensively abroad but spent a great deal of time in her caravan in the Yorkshire Dales. Dorothy had a great love of the gypsies and their Romany culture, and would go out of her way to spend time with them.

Temple Sowerby

Acorn Bank, Temple Sowerby

Sadly, Dorothy and Noel had only been married eleven years when Noel succumbed to a kidney complaint thought to be from injuries sustained during WWI, leaving Dorothy bereft. She did marry again, this time to a man she had known for some time, Alfred Charles Vowles. Strangely, she insisted he change his surname to Phillips and so she remained a Phillips till the end of her life. She died on 20th November 1967 and her ashes rest together with those of Noel and Alfred in the vault at Temple Sowerby churchyard.

Acorn Bank was left to the National Trust and the grounds are reputed to have the north of England's largest collection of medicinal and culinary herbs. Beautiful walks take you through the woodland and along the beck past the old water mill. The footpath alongside the beck passes under the Settle to Carlisle line at Crowdundle Viaduct.

Culgaith and New Biggin

New Biggin, Cumbria

It wasn't intended that the village of Culgaith should have a station but pressure from local landowners and the Church saw that one was built in 1880, four years after the commencement of passenger services on the line. A level crossing and signal box was installed at the time. The station is now in private ownership and the signal box is still manned and controls the level crossing.

Ribblehead Viaduct

Signal Box, Culgaith

Little Salkeld

Little Salkeld viaduct, sometimes known as Dodd's Mill viaduct, just north of the former railway station crosses Briggle Beck with one of its seven arches. Built in 1874–5, it was one of the last structures to be completed on the S&C. Perhaps Little Salkeld's most historic feature is its working watermill. This was built in 1745 to mill local corn and with the advent of the railway this small business flourished. It is still very much in operation today.

Langwathby and Long Meg

A couple of miles east of Langwathby can be found the Druids' temple known as Long Meg and her Daughters. This Neolithic stone circle comprising sixty-six stones measures approximately seventy metres in diameter and is said to be the second largest such circle after Stonehenge. Long Meg herself, unlike the other

Little Salkeld Viaduct

Old Mill, Little Salkeld

stones, is of red sandstone and stands about six metres high and four and a half metres all the way round. Its four corners point to the four points of the compass. It dates from about 4500 BC.

Lazonby and Kirkoswald

Lazonby and Kirkoswald shared the same railway station although the people of Kirkoswald had more than a mile to walk to reach it. In so doing those same passengers would have to cross the fine stone bridge over the Eden which is still in use today and is shown in my painting in its winter clothes. The station was the busiest on the line for livestock and other freight.

The village of Kirkoswald is named after the Church of St Oswald, Oswald being king of Northumbria. The most unusual feature of the church, which dates back to the twelfth century, is the nineteenth-century bell tower which stands high on the hill top, 200yds from the church.

Eden Gorge

Eden Gorge

Armathwaite

Another attractive Cumbrian village is Armathwaite, well known for its walks around the Eden Gorge and also its salmon fishing. The typical Midland Railway signal box closed in 1983 but was restored by the FoSC and completed in 1992, being their first signal box restoration and completed in its original paint scheme of yellow.

Wetheral

Wetheral is a small hamlet just south-east of Carlisle and my painting is of the
Priory gatehouse which dates from the fifteenth century and is the only remaining
part of what would have been a much more imposing building. Founded in 1106,
the Priory was dedicated to the Holy Trinity and St Constantine.

Carlisle (The Border City)

This pleasant city, well worth a visit, dates from long before the Roman conquest. Carlisle has had a turbulent past, especially with regard to its tug o' war history between England and Scotland.

In the ninth century the Danes laid siege to it and in 1093 the Castle was founded by William II. Mary, Queen of Scots was incarcerated in the castle for about two months in 1658 after her abdication.

The twin drum towers of the Citadel were begun as a fortress in 1541. The Citadel used its East Tower and a civil court with a criminal court was housed in the West Tower. It has recently undergone restoration and the West Tower is now open to the public. The name 'Citadel' was given to the Railway Station which was built in 1847.

The pedestrianised square houses the old Town Hall; built in 1717 it now houses the tourist information centre. In front of the old Town Hall stands the seventeenth-century Market Cross.

Citadel Station,
Carlisle

*Carlisle Town Hall
Square*

Locomotives of the Line

Compound 4-4-0 Locomotive

Designed by S. W. Johnson and introduced in 1902, this locomotive was much more powerful than its predecessors. Five were initially built and the design was perpetuated with modifications by R. M. Deeley from 1905. This design was so successful that it was adopted by the LMS in 1923 as the foremost express passenger locomotive.

Midland Compound Locomotive

Fowler 0-6-0 Freight Locomotive

*Fowler Goods
Locomotive*

Henry Fowler, who had become locomotive engineer following the resignation of
Deeley, set about producing a more powerful 0-6-0 goods locomotive capable of
handling increasing freight traffic. This locomotive was introduced in 1911 and
proved to be very reliable and cheap to run. Their relatively large driving wheels
endowed them with a fine turn of speed, so much so that they could be often seen
on excursion trains. Again, this design was adopted as the main freight locomotive
of the LMS.

*Royal Scot
Locomotive*

Rebuilt 'Royal Scot' Class Locomotive

When Henry Fowler was appointed chief mechanical engineer of the LMS in 1925, the relatively small express locomotives of the Midland Railway were becoming inadequate. Fowler was charged with producing a much larger, more powerful engine, and in 1927 his 'Royal Scot' class engines appeared. In 1943, Fowler's successor William Stanier rebuilt this class of engine into one of the most efficient designs seen on British railways. In this guise this class remained in service almost to the end of steam. My painting shows the final design of this class.

Acknowledgements

Day Night Print for scanning. John Gardner Photography. Mark Rand (former Chairman of FoSCL) Joel Walker, sculptress W. R. (Bill) Mitchell, author, for his informative chat, and my dear wife Judith for her patience during the compilation of this book.

Bibliography

1   *Historic Railway Disasters* – O S Nock, Ian Allan Ltd 1966

2   *Settle-Carlisle Railway* – W R Mitchell & David Joy, Dalesman 1966

3   *D.U.R. A Memoir* – Wilfred J Halliday, Lund Humphreys,
    The Country Press, 1969

4   *The Scenic Settle & Carlisle Railway* – Donald Binns, Wyvern
    Publications 1972

5   *To Kill a Railway* – Stan Abbott, Leading Edge Press 1986

6   *Castles of Cumbria* – M J Jackson, Carel Press 1990

7   *Mile by Mile of the S & C* – W R Mitchell, Castleberg 1997

8   *One Hundred Tales of the S & C* – W R Mitchell, Castleberg 2000

9   *Railways of the Yorkshire Dales* – Michael Blakemore, Atlantic 2001

10 *The Settle & Carlisle* – David J Williams, Past and Present
    Publications 2010

Let the daisies grow as they will,
Purple crocus and daffodil;
Near by plant a fragrant lime,
So a thrush may stay in the evening time.
Bring the children to pick the flowers,
And tell them between the April showers,
'Here lies a lover of rain and sun,
Loving and loved by everyone;
Who left these beautiful dales to find
The dales where the heavenly rivers wind'

Dorothy Una Ratcliffe